Vegetarian Anti-Inflammatory Diet Cookbook

Marion Oliver

Disclaimer

Please bear in mind that the information in this book is strictly educational. The data presented here is claimed to be credible and trustworthy. The author provides no implied or explicit assurance of accuracy for specific individual instances.

It is important that you consult with a skilled practitioner, such as your doctor, before initiating any diet or lifestyle changes. The information in this book should not be used in place of expert advice or professional assistance.

The author, publisher, and distributor fully disclaim any and all liability, loss, damage, or risk suffered by anybody who relies on the information in this book, whether directly or indirectly.

All intellectual property rights are intact. The content in this book should not be copied in any way, mechanically, electronically, by photocopying, or by any other means available.

CONTENTS

Introduction

In a world where the pace of life seems to be constantly accelerating and demands on our time and attention are ever-increasing, the importance of maintaining good health is paramount. The choices we make regarding our diet play a crucial role in determining our overall well-being. Embracing a healthier lifestyle is not just a trend; it is a conscious decision to invest in our long-term health and vitality.

One compelling avenue towards achieving and sustaining a healthier lifestyle is the adoption of a vegetarian anti-inflammatory diet. This dietary approach goes beyond mere weight management; it focuses on harnessing the power of plant-based nutrition to combat inflammation—a silent culprit that can significantly impact our health.

Inflammation is a natural and essential response by the body to injury or infection. However, when inflammation becomes chronic, it can contribute to a myriad of health issues, including cardiovascular disease, arthritis, and even certain types of cancers. A vegetarian anti-inflammatory diet stands out as an effective strategy to counteract this persistent inflammation.

The emphasis on plant-based foods in this dietary approach is rooted in the anti-inflammatory properties found in fruits, vegetables, whole grains, legumes, nuts, and seeds. These plant-derived foods are rich in antioxidants, phytochemicals, and other bioactive compounds that not only neutralize free radicals but also help regulate the body's inflammatory responses. By choosing a vegetarian anti-inflammatory diet, individuals are not only making a conscious effort to reduce inflammation but are also unlocking a plethora of nutritional benefits for their overall health.

Before delving into the specifics of a vegetarian anti-inflammatory diet, it's crucial to grasp the concept of inflammation and its far-reaching effects on health. Inflammation is the body's natural defense mechanism, involving the immune system's response to injury or infection. However, when the inflammatory response becomes chronic, it can lead to tissue damage and contribute to the development of various chronic diseases.

Chronic inflammation has been implicated in conditions such as atherosclerosis, diabetes, autoimmune disorders, and neurodegenerative diseases. By understanding the mechanisms behind inflammation, individuals can make informed choices about their diet to mitigate its adverse effects on their health.

Plant-based nutrition has gained widespread recognition for its ability to promote overall health and well-being. The benefits of plant-centric diets extend beyond the prevention of chronic diseases; they encompass weight management, improved digestion, enhanced energy levels, and even a positive impact on mental health.

The array of nutrients found in plant-based foods, including vitamins, minerals, fiber, and phytochemicals, contribute to a robust immune system and efficient physiological functions. The inherent anti-inflammatory properties of many plant foods make them a natural choice for those seeking to address inflammation and promote a healthier lifestyle.

Embarking on a journey to adopt a vegetarian anti-inflammatory diet is not just about restriction; it is an opportunity to explore a diverse and delicious world of plant-based culinary delights. This cookbook is designed to be a guide and companion on this transformative journey, offering a rich collection of recipes that prioritize health without compromising on taste.
Through carefully crafted and nutritionally balanced recipes, this cookbook aims to demonstrate that choosing a vegetarian anti-inflammatory diet can be both enjoyable and sustainable. Whether you are a seasoned chef or a novice in the kitchen, the recipes provided will inspire you to experiment with a variety of plant-based ingredients, creating meals that nourish your body and tantalize your taste buds.

In conclusion, embracing a healthier lifestyle through a vegetarian anti-inflammatory diet is a proactive step towards cultivating long-lasting well-being. By understanding the impact of inflammation on health, appreciating the power of plant-based nutrition, and embarking on a culinary journey with the help of this cookbook, individuals can transform their health and savor the benefits of a lifestyle that nourishes the body and soul.

Chapter 1: Foundations of a Vegetarian Anti-Inflammatory Diet

In the pursuit of optimal health and well-being, the foundations of a diet play a pivotal role. The first chapter of the guide on a Vegetarian Anti-Inflammatory Diet lays the groundwork for understanding the principles that govern this dietary approach. This chapter serves as a comprehensive introduction to the core concepts, the rationale behind choosing a vegetarian path, and the fundamental principles of an anti-inflammatory lifestyle.

Understanding Inflammation

Before delving into the specifics of a Vegetarian Anti-Inflammatory Diet, it is essential to comprehend the concept of inflammation. Inflammation is a natural and necessary response of the immune system to injury or infection. However, chronic inflammation, often triggered by poor dietary choices and lifestyle factors, is associated with various health issues, including cardiovascular diseases, autoimmune disorders, and even certain cancers. This chapter elucidates the difference between acute and chronic inflammation, emphasizing the need to address the latter through dietary modifications.

The Vegetarian Advantage

The decision to adopt a vegetarian diet is rooted in both ethical and health considerations. This section explores the benefits of a vegetarian lifestyle, showcasing how plant-based diets can contribute to overall health and well-being. By examining scientific studies and nutritional research, the chapter establishes the vegetarian advantage in reducing inflammation and promoting longevity.

The Anti-Inflammatory Approach

Transitioning into the core theme of the guide, this section outlines the principles of an anti-inflammatory diet. It introduces readers to inflammation-modulating foods and elucidates how they can positively impact the body's inflammatory response. From omega-3 fatty acids to antioxidants found abundantly in plant-based foods, the chapter provides a comprehensive overview of the components that contribute to an anti-inflammatory dietary approach.

Key Nutrients in a Vegetarian Anti-Inflammatory Diet

To lay a solid foundation for readers embarking on this dietary journey, the chapter delves into the key nutrients that play a crucial role in mitigating inflammation. These include but are not limited to:

- **Omega-3 Fatty Acids**: Found in abundance in sources like flaxseeds, walnuts, and chia seeds, omega-3 fatty acids are potent anti-inflammatory agents. The chapter elucidates the importance of incorporating these essential fats into the diet and suggests practical ways to do so.
- **Antioxidants**: Fruits and vegetables are rich in antioxidants, which combat oxidative stress and inflammation. The chapter provides a comprehensive list of antioxidant-rich foods, encouraging readers to diversify their plant-based intake for optimal health benefits.
- **Phytonutrients**: The vibrant colors of fruits and vegetables often signify the presence of phytonutrients, compounds with anti-inflammatory properties. This section explains the importance of incorporating a rainbow of plant foods to maximize the intake of these beneficial compounds.

Breakfast

Quinoa Breakfast Bowl with Mixed Berries

- **Total Time:** 20 minutes
- **Servings:** 2

Ingredients:
- 1 cup cooked quinoa
- 1 cup mixed berries (strawberries, blueberries, raspberries)
- 1 tablespoon honey or maple syrup
- 2 tablespoons chopped nuts (almonds, walnuts)
- 1/2 cup Greek yogurt
- 1 teaspoon chia seeds
- Fresh mint leaves for garnish

Directions:
1. In a bowl, layer cooked quinoa.
2. Top with mixed berries and drizzle with honey or maple syrup.
3. Sprinkle chopped nuts and chia seeds over the berries.
4. Add a dollop of Greek yogurt on the side.
5. Garnish with fresh mint leaves.
6. Serve and enjoy!

Nutritional Information:
- Calories: 300 per serving
- Protein: 12g
- Fiber: 8g
- Fat: 8g
- Carbohydrates: 45g

Avocado and Tomato Toast with Flaxseeds

- **Total Time:** 10 minutes
- **Servings:** 2

Ingredients:
- 2 slices whole-grain bread
- 1 ripe avocado, mashed
- 1 large tomato, sliced

- 1 tablespoon ground flaxseeds
- Salt and pepper to taste
- Red pepper flakes (optional)

Directions:
1. Toast the slices of bread to your liking.
2. Spread mashed avocado evenly on each slice.
3. Place tomato slices on top of the avocado.
4. Sprinkle ground flaxseeds, salt, and pepper.
5. Add a dash of red pepper flakes if desired.
6. Serve immediately.

Nutritional Information:
- Calories: 220 per serving
- Protein: 6g
- Fiber: 8g
- Fat: 15g
- Carbohydrates: 20g

Chia Seed Pudding with Almond Milk and Fresh Fruit

- **Total Time:** 4 hours (including chilling time)
- **Servings:** 4

Ingredients:
- 1/2 cup chia seeds
- 2 cups unsweetened almond milk
- 1 teaspoon vanilla extract
- 1 tablespoon maple syrup
- Fresh fruit for topping (berries, kiwi, mango)

Directions:
1. In a bowl, mix chia seeds, almond milk, vanilla extract, and maple syrup.
2. Stir well and refrigerate for at least 4 hours or overnight.
3. Before serving, stir the pudding to avoid clumps.
4. Spoon into serving bowls and top with fresh fruit.
5. Enjoy this nutritious pudding!

Nutritional Information:
- Calories: 150 per serving
- Protein: 5g

- Fiber: 10g
- Fat: 8g
- Carbohydrates: 15g

Spinach and Mushroom Omelette

- **Total Time:** 15 minutes
- **Servings:** 1

Ingredients:
- 2 large eggs
- 1/2 cup fresh spinach, chopped
- 1/4 cup mushrooms, sliced
- 1 tablespoon feta cheese, crumbled
- Salt and pepper to taste
- Cooking spray or olive oil for the pan

Directions:
1. In a bowl, whisk the eggs and season with salt and pepper.
2. Heat a non-stick pan over medium heat and add cooking spray or olive oil.
3. Add mushrooms to the pan and sauté until softened.
4. Add chopped spinach and cook until wilted.
5. Pour the whisked eggs over the vegetables.
6. Once the edges set, sprinkle feta cheese on one side and fold the omelette.
7. Cook for another minute until the cheese melts.
8. Slide onto a plate and serve.

Nutritional Information:
- Calories: 250 per serving
- Protein: 20g
- Fiber: 3g
- Fat: 16g
- Carbohydrates: 5g

Sweet Potato and Black Bean Breakfast Burrito

- **Total Time:** 30 minutes
- **Servings:** 2

Ingredients:
- 2 whole-grain tortillas

- 1 medium sweet potato, diced and roasted
- 1/2 cup black beans, cooked
- 1 avocado, sliced
- Salsa and cilantro for topping
- Salt and pepper to taste

Directions:
1. Roast diced sweet potatoes in the oven until tender.
2. Warm tortillas in a pan or microwave.
3. Layer sweet potatoes, black beans, and avocado slices on each tortilla.
4. Add salt and pepper to taste.
5. Top with salsa and cilantro.
6. Fold into a burrito and serve.

Nutritional Information:
- Calories: 380 per serving
- Protein: 10g
- Fiber: 12g
- Fat: 15g
- Carbohydrates: 55g

Blueberry and Almond Butter Smoothie Bowl

- **Total Time:** 10 minutes
- **Servings:** 1

Ingredients:
- 1 cup frozen blueberries
- 1 banana, sliced
- 1/2 cup almond milk
- 1 tablespoon almond butter
- 1/4 cup granola
- Chia seeds and sliced almonds for topping

Directions:
1. Blend blueberries, banana, almond milk, and almond butter until smooth.
2. Pour into a bowl and top with granola, chia seeds, and sliced almonds.
3. Customize with additional toppings if desired.
4. Enjoy this nutrient-packed smoothie bowl!

Nutritional Information:
- Calories: 350 per serving
- Protein: 8g
- Fiber: 10g
- Fat: 15g
- Carbohydrates: 50g

Turmeric Golden Milk Overnight Oats

- **Total Time:** 4 hours (including chilling time)
- **Servings:** 2

Ingredients:
- 1 cup rolled oats
- 1 cup unsweetened almond milk
- 1/2 teaspoon ground turmeric
- 1/4 teaspoon ground cinnamon
- 1 tablespoon maple syrup
- Sliced banana and chopped nuts for topping

Directions:
1. In a jar, mix oats, almond milk, turmeric, cinnamon, and maple syrup.
2. Stir well, cover, and refrigerate for at least 4 hours or overnight.
3. Before serving, stir the oats and add more almond milk if needed.
4. Top with sliced banana and chopped nuts.
5. Enjoy these flavorful golden milk overnight oats!

Nutritional Information:
- Calories: 220 per serving
- Protein: 6g
- Fiber: 8g
- Fat: 5g
- Carbohydrates: 40g

Vegan Banana Walnut Pancakes

- **Total Time:** 20 minutes
- **Servings:** 2

Ingredients:
- 1 cup whole wheat flour

- 1 tablespoon baking powder
- 1 ripe banana, mashed
- 1 cup almond milk
- 1/4 cup chopped walnuts
- 1 tablespoon maple syrup
- 1 teaspoon vanilla extract
- Cooking spray or coconut oil for the pan

Directions:

1. In a bowl, whisk together flour and baking powder.
2. Add mashed banana, almond milk, chopped walnuts, maple syrup, and vanilla extract. Mix until just combined.
3. Heat a pan over medium heat, add cooking spray or coconut oil.
4. Pour 1/4 cup of batter for each pancake onto the pan.
5. Cook until bubbles form on the surface, then flip and cook until golden brown.
6. Serve with additional banana slices and maple syrup.

Nutritional Information:

- Calories: 350 per serving
- Protein: 8g
- Fiber: 6g
- Fat: 10g
- Carbohydrates: 60g

Mediterranean Chickpea Scramble

- **Total Time:** 15 minutes
- **Servings:** 2

Ingredients:

- 1 can (15 oz) chickpeas, drained and rinsed
- 1 tablespoon olive oil
- 1/2 red bell pepper, diced
- 1/2 red onion, diced
- 2 cloves garlic, minced
- 1 teaspoon ground cumin
- 1 teaspoon smoked paprika
- Salt and pepper to taste
- Fresh parsley for garnish

Directions:
1. In a pan, heat olive oil over medium heat.
2. Add diced bell pepper and onion, sauté until softened.
3. Stir in minced garlic, ground cumin, smoked paprika, salt, and pepper.
4. Add chickpeas to the pan, and cook until heated through.
5. Garnish with fresh parsley and serve warm.

Nutritional Information:
- Calories: 280 per serving
- Protein: 10g
- Fiber: 8g
- Fat: 10g
- Carbohydrates: 40g

Berry and Spinach Breakfast Smoothie

- **Total Time:** 10 minutes
- **Servings:** 1

Ingredients:
- 1 cup mixed berries (strawberries, blueberries, raspberries)
- 1 banana, frozen
- 1 cup fresh spinach
- 1/2 cup almond milk
- 1 tablespoon chia seeds
- 1 tablespoon almond butter
- Ice cubes (optional)

Directions:
1. In a blender, combine mixed berries, frozen banana, fresh spinach, almond milk, chia seeds, and almond butter.
2. Blend until smooth and creamy.
3. Add ice cubes if a colder consistency is desired.
4. Pour into a glass and enjoy this refreshing smoothie!

Nutritional Information:
- Calories: 300 per serving
- Protein: 8g
- Fiber: 12g
- Fat: 10g
- Carbohydrates: 45g

Coconut Yogurt Parfait with Granola and Berries

- **Total Time:** 10 minutes
- **Servings:** 1

Ingredients:
- 1 cup coconut yogurt
- 1/2 cup granola
- 1/2 cup mixed berries (blueberries, raspberries, strawberries)
- 1 tablespoon shredded coconut
- Drizzle of honey or maple syrup

Directions:
1. In a glass or bowl, layer coconut yogurt, granola, and mixed berries.
2. Repeat layers until the container is filled.
3. Top with shredded coconut and drizzle with honey or maple syrup.
4. Serve immediately and savor the deliciousness!

Nutritional Information:
- Calories: 380 per serving
- Protein: 10g
- Fiber: 8g
- Fat: 15g
- Carbohydrates: 55g

Cinnamon Raisin Quinoa Porridge

- **Total Time:** 15 minutes
- **Servings:** 2

Ingredients:
- 1 cup cooked quinoa
- 1 cup almond milk
- 1/4 cup raisins
- 1 tablespoon maple syrup
- 1/2 teaspoon ground cinnamon
- 1/4 teaspoon vanilla extract
- Chopped nuts for topping

Directions:
1. In a saucepan, heat almond milk over medium heat.

2. Add cooked quinoa, raisins, maple syrup, ground cinnamon, and vanilla extract.
3. Stir and cook until heated through.
4. Serve in bowls and top with chopped nuts.

Nutritional Information:
- Calories: 220 per serving
- Protein: 5g
- Fiber: 4g
- Fat: 5g
- Carbohydrates: 40g

Green Pea and Mint Frittata

- **Total Time:** 25 minutes
- **Servings:** 4

Ingredients:
- 6 large eggs
- 1 cup fresh or frozen green peas
- 1/4 cup feta cheese, crumbled
- 2 tablespoons fresh mint, chopped
- Salt and pepper to taste
- 1 tablespoon olive oil

Directions:
1. Preheat the oven broiler.
2. In a bowl, whisk eggs and season with salt and pepper.
3. Heat olive oil in an oven-proof skillet over medium heat.
4. Add green peas and sauté for 2-3 minutes.
5. Pour the whisked eggs over the peas, sprinkle with feta and chopped mint.
6. Cook on the stove for 5 minutes, then transfer to the broiler for an additional 5 minutes until the top is set.
7. Slice into wedges and serve.

Nutritional Information:
- Calories: 180 per serving
- Protein: 12g
- Fiber: 3g
- Fat: 10g
- Carbohydrates: 10g

Mango and Coconut Chia Seed Parfait

- **Total Time:** 4 hours (including chilling time)
- **Servings:** 2

Ingredients:
- 1 cup mango, diced
- 1 cup coconut yogurt
- 1/4 cup chia seeds
- 1 tablespoon shredded coconut
- 1 tablespoon honey or agave syrup

Directions:
1. In a bowl, mix chia seeds, coconut yogurt, and honey or agave syrup.
2. Refrigerate for at least 4 hours or overnight.
3. In serving glasses, layer the chia seed mixture with diced mango.
4. Top with shredded coconut.
5. Serve chilled and enjoy this tropical parfait!

Nutritional Information:
- Calories: 280 per serving
- Protein: 6g
- Fiber: 10g
- Fat: 12g
- Carbohydrates: 35g

Sweet Potato and Kale Breakfast Hash

- **Total Time:** 30 minutes
- **Servings:** 2

Ingredients:
- 2 medium sweet potatoes, diced
- 2 cups kale, chopped
- 1 red bell pepper, diced
- 1 small red onion, diced
- 2 cloves garlic, minced
- 2 tablespoons olive oil
- 1 teaspoon smoked paprika
- Salt and pepper to taste
- Poached eggs for topping (optional)

Directions:

1. In a skillet, heat olive oil over medium heat.
2. Add diced sweet potatoes and cook until slightly softened.
3. Add red bell pepper, red onion, and minced garlic. Sauté until vegetables are tender.
4. Stir in chopped kale and cook until wilted.
5. Season with smoked paprika, salt, and pepper.
6. If desired, top with poached eggs.
7. Serve warm and enjoy this hearty breakfast hash!

Nutritional Information:

- Calories: 320 per serving
- Protein: 6g
- Fiber: 8g
- Fat: 12g
- Carbohydrates: 45g

Lunch

Lentil and Vegetable Stuffed Bell Peppers

- **Total Time:** 45 minutes
- **Servings:** 4

Ingredients:
- 4 large bell peppers, halved and seeds removed
- 1 cup cooked lentils
- 1 cup quinoa, cooked
- 1 cup cherry tomatoes, diced
- 1/2 cup red onion, finely chopped
- 1/2 cup corn kernels
- 1/2 cup black beans, drained and rinsed
- 1 teaspoon cumin
- 1 teaspoon smoked paprika
- Salt and pepper to taste
- 1 cup tomato sauce
- 1/2 cup shredded vegan cheese (optional)

Directions:
1. Preheat the oven to 375°F (190°C).
2. In a bowl, mix cooked lentils, quinoa, cherry tomatoes, red onion, corn, black beans, cumin, smoked paprika, salt, and pepper.
3. Stuff each bell pepper half with the lentil and vegetable mixture.
4. Place stuffed peppers in a baking dish and pour tomato sauce over them.
5. Cover with aluminum foil and bake for 30 minutes.
6. If using, sprinkle shredded vegan cheese on top and bake uncovered for an additional 10 minutes or until cheese is melted and bubbly.
7. Serve warm.

Nutritional Information:
- Calories: 300 per serving
- Protein: 15g
- Fiber: 10g
- Fat: 5g
- Carbohydrates: 50g

Greek Salad with Chickpea Patties

- **Total Time:** 30 minutes
- **Servings:** 2

Ingredients:
- 1 cup cherry tomatoes, halved
- 1 cucumber, diced
- 1 cup Kalamata olives, pitted and sliced
- 1/2 cup red onion, thinly sliced
- 1 cup chickpea patties (store-bought or homemade)
- 1/2 cup feta cheese, crumbled
- 2 tablespoons extra virgin olive oil
- 1 tablespoon red wine vinegar
- 1 teaspoon dried oregano
- Salt and pepper to taste

Directions:
1. In a large bowl, combine cherry tomatoes, cucumber, Kalamata olives, and red onion.
2. In a separate pan, cook chickpea patties according to package instructions.
3. Once cooked, slice the chickpea patties into bite-sized pieces.
4. Add chickpea patty slices to the salad.
5. In a small bowl, whisk together olive oil, red wine vinegar, dried oregano, salt, and pepper.
6. Drizzle the dressing over the salad and toss gently.
7. Sprinkle crumbled feta cheese on top.
8. Serve immediately.

Nutritional Information:
- Calories: 400 per serving
- Protein: 15g
- Fiber: 8g
- Fat: 20g
- Carbohydrates: 40g

Quinoa and Black Bean Buddha Bowl

- **Total Time:** 25 minutes
- **Servings:** 2

Ingredients:
- 1 cup quinoa, cooked
- 1 cup black beans, cooked
- 1 cup broccoli florets, steamed
- 1 carrot, julienned
- 1/2 avocado, sliced
- 2 tablespoons tahini
- 1 tablespoon soy sauce
- 1 teaspoon sesame oil
- Sesame seeds for garnish

Directions:
1. In two bowls, arrange cooked quinoa, black beans, steamed broccoli, julienned carrot, and sliced avocado.
2. In a small bowl, whisk together tahini, soy sauce, and sesame oil to make the dressing.
3. Drizzle the dressing over the Buddha bowls.
4. Garnish with sesame seeds.
5. Serve and enjoy this nutritious and flavorful bowl.

Nutritional Information:
- Calories: 450 per serving
- Protein: 15g
- Fiber: 12g
- Fat: 15g
- Carbohydrates: 60g

Roasted Vegetable Wrap with Hummus

- **Total Time:** 30 minutes
- **Servings:** 2

Ingredients:
- 2 whole-grain wraps
- 1 cup mixed bell peppers, sliced
- 1 zucchini, sliced

- 1 cup cherry tomatoes, halved
- 1 tablespoon olive oil
- Salt and pepper to taste
- 1/2 cup hummus
- Fresh basil leaves for garnish

Directions:
1. Preheat the oven to 400°F (200°C).
2. Toss sliced bell peppers, zucchini, and cherry tomatoes with olive oil, salt, and pepper.
3. Roast the vegetables in the oven for 20 minutes or until tender.
4. Spread hummus over each whole-grain wrap.
5. Place a generous portion of roasted vegetables on each wrap.
6. Garnish with fresh basil leaves.
7. Roll into wraps and serve.

Nutritional Information:
- Calories: 320 per serving
- Protein: 10g
- Fiber: 8g
- Fat: 15g
- Carbohydrates: 40g

Spinach and Feta Stuffed Mushrooms

- **Total Time:** 20 minutes
- **Servings:** 4

Ingredients:
- 16 large mushrooms, cleaned and stems removed
- 2 cups fresh spinach, chopped
- 1/2 cup feta cheese, crumbled
- 2 cloves garlic, minced
- 1 tablespoon olive oil
- Salt and pepper to taste
- Fresh parsley for garnish

Directions:
1. Preheat the oven to 375°F (190°C).
2. In a pan, sauté chopped spinach and minced garlic in olive oil until wilted.
3. Mix in crumbled feta cheese, salt, and pepper.

4. Stuff each mushroom cap with the spinach and feta mixture.
5. Place stuffed mushrooms on a baking sheet.
6. Bake for 15 minutes or until mushrooms are tender.
7. Garnish with fresh parsley and serve warm.

Nutritional Information:
- Calories: 120 per serving
- Protein: 6g
- Fiber: 3g
- Fat: 8g
- Carbohydrates: 7g

Pesto Zucchini Noodles with Cherry Tomatoes
- **Total Time:** 15 minutes
- **Servings:** 2

Ingredients:
- 2 medium zucchinis, spiralized
- 1 cup cherry tomatoes, halved
- 1/4 cup pine nuts, toasted
- 2 tablespoons vegan pesto
- 1 tablespoon nutritional yeast
- Salt and pepper to taste
- Fresh basil leaves for garnish

Directions:
1. In a pan, lightly sauté zucchini noodles until just tender.
2. Add cherry tomatoes, pine nuts, vegan pesto, and nutritional yeast.
3. Toss until well combined and heated through.
4. Season with salt and pepper to taste.
5. Garnish with fresh basil leaves.
6. Serve warm and enjoy this quick and flavorful dish.

Nutritional Information:
- Calories: 200 per serving
- Protein: 5g
- Fiber: 5g
- Fat: 15g
- Carbohydrates: 15g

Chickpea and Avocado Salad

- **Total Time:** 15 minutes
- **Servings:** 2

Ingredients:

- 1 can (15 oz) chickpeas, drained and rinsed
- 1 avocado, diced
- 1 cup cucumber, diced
- 1/2 cup cherry tomatoes, halved
- 1/4 cup red onion, finely chopped
- 2 tablespoons fresh cilantro, chopped
- Juice of 1 lemon
- 1 tablespoon extra virgin olive oil
- Salt and pepper to taste

Directions:

1. In a bowl, combine chickpeas, diced avocado, cucumber, cherry tomatoes, red onion, and cilantro.
2. In a small bowl, whisk together lemon juice, olive oil, salt, and pepper.
3. Pour the dressing over the salad and toss gently to combine.
4. Serve chilled or at room temperature.

Nutritional Information:

- Calories: 320 per serving
- Protein: 10g
- Fiber: 12g
- Fat: 18g
- Carbohydrates: 35g

Cauliflower and Chickpea Curry

- **Total Time:** 40 minutes
- **Servings:** 4

Ingredients:

- 1 cauliflower, cut into florets
- 1 can (15 oz) chickpeas, drained and rinsed
- 1 onion, finely chopped
- 2 cloves garlic, minced
- 1 can (14 oz) diced tomatoes

- 1 can (14 oz) coconut milk
- 2 tablespoons curry powder
- 1 teaspoon ground cumin
- 1 teaspoon ground coriander
- Salt and pepper to taste
- Fresh cilantro for garnish
- Cooked rice for serving

Directions:
1. In a large pan, sauté chopped onion and minced garlic until softened.
2. Add cauliflower florets and cook for 5 minutes.
3. Stir in chickpeas, diced tomatoes, coconut milk, curry powder, cumin, coriander, salt, and pepper.
4. Simmer for 20-25 minutes or until the cauliflower is tender.
5. Serve over cooked rice and garnish with fresh cilantro.

Nutritional Information:
- Calories: 350 per serving
- Protein: 10g
- Fiber: 12g
- Fat: 15g
- Carbohydrates: 45g

Caprese Salad with Balsamic Glaze

- **Total Time:** 15 minutes
- **Servings:** 2

Ingredients:
- 2 large tomatoes, sliced
- 1 ball fresh mozzarella, sliced
- Fresh basil leaves
- Balsamic glaze
- Extra virgin olive oil
- Salt and pepper to taste

Directions:
1. Arrange tomato and mozzarella slices on a serving platter.
2. Tuck fresh basil leaves between the tomato and mozzarella slices.
3. Drizzle with balsamic glaze and olive oil.
4. Season with salt and pepper to taste.
5. Serve as a refreshing Caprese salad.

Nutritional Information:
- Calories: 250 per serving
- Protein: 12g
- Fiber: 3g
- Fat: 20g
- Carbohydrates: 10g

Sweet Potato and Quinoa Salad with Lemon Tahini Dressing

- **Total Time:** 30 minutes
- **Servings:** 4

Ingredients:
- 2 sweet potatoes, diced
- 1 cup quinoa, cooked
- 1 cup cherry tomatoes, halved
- 1/2 cucumber, diced
- 1/4 cup red onion, finely chopped
- 1/4 cup fresh parsley, chopped
- 1/4 cup tahini
- Juice of 1 lemon
- 2 tablespoons olive oil
- Salt and pepper to taste

Directions:
1. Roast diced sweet potatoes in the oven until tender.
2. In a large bowl, combine cooked quinoa, roasted sweet potatoes, cherry tomatoes, cucumber, red onion, and fresh parsley.
3. In a small bowl, whisk together tahini, lemon juice, olive oil, salt, and pepper.
4. Pour the dressing over the salad and toss gently.
5. Serve chilled or at room temperature.

Nutritional Information:
- Calories: 320 per serving
- Protein: 8g
- Fiber: 8g
- Fat: 15g
- Carbohydrates: 40g

Mediterranean Stuffed Eggplant

- **Total Time:** 45 minutes
- **Servings:** 2

Ingredients:
- 2 large eggplants, halved
- 1 can (15 oz) chickpeas, drained and rinsed
- 1 cup cherry tomatoes, halved
- 1/2 cup Kalamata olives, pitted and sliced
- 1/4 cup red onion, finely chopped
- 2 cloves garlic, minced
- 2 tablespoons fresh oregano, chopped
- 2 tablespoons olive oil
- Salt and pepper to taste
- Crumbled feta cheese for garnish (optional)

Directions:
1. Preheat the oven to 375°F (190°C).
2. Scoop out the center of each eggplant half, leaving a shell.
3. In a bowl, mix chickpeas, cherry tomatoes, Kalamata olives, red onion, garlic, oregano, olive oil, salt, and pepper.
4. Stuff each eggplant half with the chickpea mixture.
5. Place stuffed eggplants in a baking dish and bake for 30 minutes.
6. If desired, sprinkle crumbled feta cheese on top and bake for an additional 10 minutes or until golden.
7. Serve warm.

Nutritional Information:
- Calories: 280 per serving
- Protein: 10g
- Fiber: 12g
- Fat: 15g
- Carbohydrates: 35g

Broccoli and White Bean Soup

- **Total Time:** 30 minutes
- **Servings:** 4

Ingredients:

- 2 cups broccoli florets
- 1 can (15 oz) white beans, drained and rinsed
- 1 onion, chopped
- 2 cloves garlic, minced
- 4 cups vegetable broth
- 1 teaspoon dried thyme
- Salt and pepper to taste
- 2 tablespoons olive oil
- Lemon wedges for serving

Directions:

1. In a pot, sauté chopped onion and minced garlic in olive oil until softened.
2. Add broccoli florets, white beans, vegetable broth, dried thyme, salt, and pepper.
3. Simmer for 15-20 minutes or until broccoli is tender.
4. Use an immersion blender to blend the soup to your desired consistency.
5. Serve hot with a squeeze of lemon.

Nutritional Information:

- Calories: 180 per serving
- Protein: 8g
- Fiber: 8g
- Fat: 7g
- Carbohydrates: 25g

Spinach and Lentil Soup

- **Total Time:** 40 minutes
- **Servings:** 4

Ingredients:

- 1 cup dried green lentils, rinsed
- 1 onion, chopped
- 2 carrots, diced
- 2 celery stalks, diced
- 3 cloves garlic, minced

- 4 cups vegetable broth
- 2 cups fresh spinach, chopped
- 1 teaspoon ground cumin
- 1/2 teaspoon smoked paprika
- Salt and pepper to taste
- 2 tablespoons olive oil
- Lemon wedges for serving

Directions:

1. In a large pot, sauté chopped onion, diced carrots, diced celery, and minced garlic in olive oil until softened.
2. Add green lentils, vegetable broth, ground cumin, smoked paprika, salt, and pepper.
3. Simmer for 25-30 minutes or until lentils are tender.
4. Stir in chopped spinach and cook until wilted.
5. Serve hot with a squeeze of lemon.

Nutritional Information:

- Calories: 220 per serving
- Protein: 12g
- Fiber: 10g
- Fat: 7g
- Carbohydrates: 30g

Vegan Caesar Salad with Crispy Chickpeas

- **Total Time:** 20 minutes
- **Servings:** 2

Ingredients:

- 1 head romaine lettuce, chopped
- 1 cup cherry tomatoes, halved
- 1/2 cup cucumber, sliced
- 1/4 cup red onion, thinly sliced
- 1 cup crispy chickpeas (store-bought or homemade)
- 1/4 cup vegan Caesar dressing
- 2 tablespoons nutritional yeast
- Lemon wedges for serving

Directions:

1. In a large bowl, combine chopped romaine lettuce, cherry tomatoes, sliced cucumber, and thinly sliced red onion.
2. Toss in crispy chickpeas.
3. Drizzle with vegan Caesar dressing and toss until well coated.
4. Sprinkle nutritional yeast over the salad.
5. Serve with lemon wedges for an extra burst of flavor.

Nutritional Information:

- Calories: 250 per serving
- Protein: 8g
- Fiber: 8g
- Fat: 15g
- Carbohydrates: 25g

Roasted Vegetable and Quinoa Stuffed Portobello Mushrooms

- **Total Time:** 35 minutes
- **Servings:** 2

Ingredients:

- 4 large portobello mushrooms, stems removed
- 1 cup quinoa, cooked
- 1 cup cherry tomatoes, halved
- 1/2 cup red bell pepper, diced
- 1/4 cup red onion, finely chopped
- 2 cloves garlic, minced
- 2 tablespoons balsamic glaze
- 2 tablespoons olive oil
- Salt and pepper to taste
- Fresh basil leaves for garnish

Directions:

1. Preheat the oven to 375°F (190°C).
2. Place portobello mushrooms on a baking sheet.
3. In a bowl, mix cooked quinoa, cherry tomatoes, diced red bell pepper, red onion, minced garlic, balsamic glaze, olive oil, salt, and pepper.
4. Stuff each portobello mushroom with the quinoa mixture.
5. Bake for 20-25 minutes or until mushrooms are tender.
6. Garnish with fresh basil leaves and serve warm.

Nutritional Information:

- Calories: 320 per serving
- Protein: 10g
- Fiber: 8g
- Fat: 15g
- Carbohydrates: 40g

Dinner

Eggplant and Spinach Lasagna

- **Total Time:** 1 hour
- **Servings:** 6

Ingredients:

- 1 large eggplant, sliced
- 2 cups fresh spinach
- 1 can (15 oz) crushed tomatoes
- 1 cup tomato sauce
- 2 cloves garlic, minced
- 1 teaspoon dried oregano
- 1 teaspoon dried basil
- Salt and pepper to taste
- 2 cups ricotta cheese
- 1 cup mozzarella cheese, shredded
- 1/2 cup Parmesan cheese, grated
- Lasagna noodles, cooked according to package instructions

Directions:

1. Preheat the oven to 375°F (190°C).
2. In a pan, sauté garlic in olive oil until fragrant.
3. Add crushed tomatoes, tomato sauce, oregano, basil, salt, and pepper. Simmer for 15 minutes.
4. In a separate pan, sauté sliced eggplant until tender.
5. In a baking dish, layer lasagna noodles, ricotta cheese, spinach, eggplant, and tomato sauce mixture.
6. Repeat layers, finishing with a layer of tomato sauce on top.
7. Sprinkle mozzarella and Parmesan cheese on top.
8. Bake for 30-35 minutes or until the cheese is melted and bubbly.
9. Allow to cool slightly before serving.

Nutritional Information:

- Calories: 400 per serving
- Protein: 20g
- Fiber: 6g
- Fat: 20g
- Carbohydrates: 35g

Lentil and Sweet Potato Curry

- **Total Time:** 45 minutes
- **Servings:** 4

Ingredients:
- 1 cup dried lentils, rinsed
- 2 sweet potatoes, diced
- 1 can (15 oz) coconut milk
- 1 onion, chopped
- 2 cloves garlic, minced
- 2 tablespoons red curry paste
- 1 teaspoon ground turmeric
- Salt and pepper to taste
- Fresh cilantro for garnish
- Cooked rice for serving

Directions:
1. In a pot, sauté chopped onion and minced garlic in olive oil until softened.
2. Add sweet potatoes, lentils, coconut milk, red curry paste, ground turmeric, salt, and pepper.
3. Simmer for 30 minutes or until lentils and sweet potatoes are tender.
4. Serve over cooked rice and garnish with fresh cilantro.

Nutritional Information:
- Calories: 350 per serving
- Protein: 15g
- Fiber: 10g
- Fat: 15g
- Carbohydrates: 40g

Mushroom and Spinach Stuffed Bell Peppers

- **Total Time:** 35 minutes
- **Servings:** 4

Ingredients:
- 4 large bell peppers, halved and seeds removed
- 2 cups mushrooms, chopped
- 2 cups fresh spinach, chopped
- 1 cup quinoa, cooked

- 1/2 cup onion, finely chopped
- 2 cloves garlic, minced
- 1 teaspoon dried thyme
- Salt and pepper to taste
- 1 cup tomato sauce
- 1/2 cup mozzarella cheese, shredded

Directions:

1. Preheat the oven to 375°F (190°C).
2. In a pan, sauté chopped mushrooms, spinach, onion, and garlic until softened.
3. Stir in cooked quinoa, dried thyme, salt, and pepper.
4. Place bell pepper halves in a baking dish and fill with the quinoa mixture.
5. Pour tomato sauce over the stuffed peppers.
6. Sprinkle shredded mozzarella cheese on top.
7. Bake for 20-25 minutes or until the peppers are tender.
8. Serve hot.

Nutritional Information:

- Calories: 280 per serving
- Protein: 10g
- Fiber: 8g
- Fat: 10g
- Carbohydrates: 40g

Cauliflower and Chickpea Tacos

- **Total Time:** 30 minutes
- **Servings:** 4

Ingredients:

- 1 cauliflower head, cut into florets
- 1 can (15 oz) chickpeas, drained and rinsed
- 2 tablespoons taco seasoning
- 1 tablespoon olive oil
- Salt and pepper to taste
- 8 small corn or whole wheat tortillas
- 1 cup shredded lettuce
- 1 cup cherry tomatoes, halved
- 1/2 cup red onion, finely chopped
- 1/2 cup guacamole
- Fresh cilantro for garnish

Directions:

1. Preheat the oven to 400°F (200°C).
2. Toss cauliflower florets and chickpeas with taco seasoning, olive oil, salt, and pepper.
3. Roast in the oven for 20-25 minutes or until cauliflower is golden and chickpeas are crispy.
4. Warm tortillas in a dry skillet or microwave.
5. Assemble tacos with roasted cauliflower and chickpeas, shredded lettuce, cherry tomatoes, red onion, and guacamole.
6. Garnish with fresh cilantro.
7. Serve immediately.

Nutritional Information:

- Calories: 300 per serving
- Protein: 10g
- Fiber: 8g
- Fat: 10g
- Carbohydrates: 45g

Tomato and Basil Spaghetti Squash

- **Total Time:** 40 minutes
- **Servings:** 2

Ingredients:

- 1 spaghetti squash, halved and seeds removed
- 2 tablespoons olive oil
- 3 cloves garlic, minced
- 2 cups cherry tomatoes, halved
- 1/4 cup fresh basil, chopped
- Salt and pepper to taste
- 1/4 cup grated Parmesan cheese (optional)

Directions:

1. Preheat the oven to 375°F (190°C).
2. Brush the cut sides of the spaghetti squash with olive oil and season with salt and pepper.
3. Place the squash, cut side down, on a baking sheet and roast for 30-35 minutes or until tender.
4. In a pan, sauté minced garlic in olive oil until fragrant.
5. Add cherry tomatoes and cook until softened.

6. Scrape the spaghetti squash flesh with a fork and add it to the pan with the tomatoes.
7. Toss the squash and tomatoes together until well combined.
8. Stir in chopped fresh basil.
9. If desired, sprinkle grated Parmesan cheese on top before serving.

Nutritional Information:
- Calories: 250 per serving
- Protein: 5g
- Fiber: 8g
- Fat: 15g
- Carbohydrates: 30g

Coconut Curry Quinoa Bowl

- **Total Time:** 30 minutes
- **Servings:** 4

Ingredients:
- 1 cup quinoa, cooked
- 1 can (15 oz) chickpeas, drained and rinsed
- 1 cup broccoli florets, steamed
- 1 cup carrots, julienned and steamed
- 1/2 cup coconut milk
- 2 tablespoons red curry paste
- 1 tablespoon soy sauce
- 1 tablespoon maple syrup
- 1 tablespoon lime juice
- Fresh cilantro for garnish
- Crushed peanuts for garnish (optional)

Directions:
1. In a bowl, mix cooked quinoa, chickpeas, steamed broccoli, and julienned carrots.
2. In a saucepan, whisk together coconut milk, red curry paste, soy sauce, maple syrup, and lime juice.
3. Simmer the sauce until heated through.
4. Pour the coconut curry sauce over the quinoa mixture and toss until well coated.
5. Garnish with fresh cilantro and crushed peanuts.
6. Serve warm.

Nutritional Information:
- Calories: 350 per serving
- Protein: 12g
- Fiber: 8g
- Fat: 15g
- Carbohydrates: 45g

Baked Falafel with Tahini Sauce

- **Total Time:** 45 minutes
- **Servings:** 4

Ingredients:
- 1 can (15 oz) chickpeas, drained and rinsed
- 1/2 cup fresh parsley, chopped
- 1/4 cup red onion, chopped
- 2 cloves garlic, minced
- 1 teaspoon ground cumin
- 1 teaspoon ground coriander
- Salt and pepper to taste
- 2 tablespoons olive oil
- 1/4 cup whole wheat flour
- Tahini sauce for serving

Directions:
1. Preheat the oven to 375°F (190°C).
2. In a food processor, blend chickpeas, fresh parsley, red onion, minced garlic, cumin, coriander, salt, and pepper until well combined.
3. Transfer the mixture to a bowl and stir in olive oil and whole wheat flour.
4. Form the mixture into small patties and place them on a baking sheet.
5. Bake for 25-30 minutes or until falafel is golden brown.
6. Serve with tahini sauce for dipping.

Nutritional Information:
- Calories: 200 per serving
- Protein: 8g
- Fiber: 6g
- Fat: 10g
- Carbohydrates: 25g

Ratatouille with Herbed Quinoa

- **Total Time:** 50 minutes
- **Servings:** 4

Ingredients:
- 1 eggplant, diced
- 1 zucchini, sliced
- 1 yellow bell pepper, diced
- 1 red onion, diced
- 2 cups cherry tomatoes, halved
- 3 cloves garlic, minced
- 1/4 cup olive oil
- 1 teaspoon dried thyme
- 1 teaspoon dried rosemary
- Salt and pepper to taste
- 1 cup quinoa, cooked
- Fresh basil for garnish

Directions:
1. Preheat the oven to 375°F (190°C).
2. In a large baking dish, combine diced eggplant, sliced zucchini, diced yellow bell pepper, diced red onion, cherry tomatoes, minced garlic, olive oil, dried thyme, dried rosemary, salt, and pepper.
3. Roast in the oven for 35-40 minutes or until vegetables are tender.
4. Serve the ratatouille over cooked herbed quinoa.
5. Garnish with fresh basil.

Nutritional Information:
- Calories: 300 per serving
- Protein: 8g
- Fiber: 10g
- Fat: 12g
- Carbohydrates: 45g

Stuffed Acorn Squash with Wild Rice

- **Total Time:** 1 hour
- **Servings:** 4

Ingredients:

- 2 acorn squash, halved and seeds removed
- 1 cup wild rice, cooked
- 1 cup mushrooms, chopped
- 1/2 cup celery, diced
- 1/2 cup dried cranberries
- 1/4 cup pecans, chopped
- 1 teaspoon dried sage
- 1 teaspoon dried thyme
- Salt and pepper to taste
- 2 tablespoons olive oil

Directions:

1. Preheat the oven to 375°F (190°C).
2. Place acorn squash halves in a baking dish.
3. In a bowl, mix cooked wild rice, chopped mushrooms, diced celery, dried cranberries, chopped pecans, dried sage, dried thyme, salt, and pepper.
4. Stuff each acorn squash half with the wild rice mixture.
5. Drizzle with olive oil.
6. Bake for 35-40 minutes or until the squash is tender.
7. Serve warm.

Nutritional Information:

- Calories: 320 per serving
- Protein: 7g
- Fiber: 8g
- Fat: 10g
- Carbohydrates: 55g

Vegan Lentil Meatballs with Tomato Sauce

- **Total Time:** 45 minutes
- **Servings:** 4

Ingredients:

- 1 cup dried green lentils, rinsed

- 2 cups vegetable broth
- 1 onion, finely chopped
- 2 cloves garlic, minced
- 1 cup breadcrumbs
- 1/4 cup nutritional yeast
- 1 teaspoon dried oregano
- 1 teaspoon dried basil
- Salt and pepper to taste
- 1 can (15 oz) crushed tomatoes
- Fresh parsley for garnish
- Cooked pasta for serving

Directions:
1. In a pot, cook green lentils in vegetable broth until tender.
2. In a pan, sauté chopped onion and minced garlic until softened.
3. In a food processor, blend cooked lentils, sautéed onion and garlic, breadcrumbs, nutritional yeast, dried oregano, dried basil, salt, and pepper until a dough-like consistency is formed.
4. Shape the mixture into meatballs and place them on a baking sheet.
5. Bake at 375°F (190°C) for 20-25 minutes or until golden brown.
6. In a separate pan, heat crushed tomatoes and simmer for 10 minutes.
7. Serve lentil meatballs over cooked pasta, topped with tomato sauce.
8. Garnish with fresh parsley.

Nutritional Information:
- Calories: 380 per serving
- Protein: 15g
- Fiber: 12g
- Fat: 8g
- Carbohydrates: 60g

Spicy Thai Basil Eggplant Stir-Fry

- **Total Time:** 30 minutes
- **Servings:** 3

Ingredients:
- 1 large eggplant, diced
- 2 tablespoons soy sauce
- 1 tablespoon hoisin sauce
- 1 tablespoon Sriracha sauce

- 2 tablespoons vegetable oil
- 3 cloves garlic, minced
- 1 red bell pepper, sliced
- 1 cup snap peas
- 1 cup basil leaves
- Cooked jasmine rice for serving

Directions:
1. In a bowl, mix diced eggplant with soy sauce, hoisin sauce, and Sriracha sauce.
2. Heat vegetable oil in a wok or large pan over medium-high heat.
3. Add minced garlic and sauté until fragrant.
4. Add the marinated eggplant and stir-fry for 5-7 minutes or until tender.
5. Add sliced red bell pepper and snap peas; stir-fry for an additional 3-4 minutes.
6. Stir in basil leaves until wilted.
7. Serve the stir-fry over cooked jasmine rice.

Nutritional Information:
- Calories: 280 per serving
- Protein: 5g
- Fiber: 8g
- Fat: 10g
- Carbohydrates: 45g

Butternut Squash and Black Bean Enchiladas

- **Total Time:** 1 hour
- **Servings:** 4

Ingredients:
- 1 butternut squash, peeled and diced
- 1 can (15 oz) black beans, drained and rinsed
- 1 onion, chopped
- 2 cloves garlic, minced
- 1 teaspoon ground cumin
- 1 teaspoon chili powder
- Salt and pepper to taste
- 8 whole wheat tortillas
- 2 cups enchilada sauce
- 1 cup shredded vegan cheese
- Fresh cilantro for garnish
- Avocado slices for serving

Directions:

1. Preheat the oven to 375°F (190°C).
2. Roast diced butternut squash on a baking sheet until tender.
3. In a pan, sauté chopped onion and minced garlic until softened.
4. Add black beans, ground cumin, chili powder, salt, and pepper. Cook for 5 minutes.
5. In a large bowl, mix the roasted butternut squash with the black bean mixture.
6. Spoon the filling onto each tortilla, roll them, and place them in a baking dish.
7. Pour enchilada sauce over the rolled tortillas and sprinkle with vegan cheese.
8. Bake for 25-30 minutes or until the enchiladas are bubbly and golden.
9. Garnish with fresh cilantro and serve with avocado slices.

Nutritional Information:

- Calories: 400 per serving
- Protein: 12g
- Fiber: 10g
- Fat: 15g
- Carbohydrates: 60g

Mediterranean Couscous Stuffed Peppers

- **Total Time:** 40 minutes
- **Servings:** 4

Ingredients:

- 4 bell peppers, halved and seeds removed
- 1 cup couscous, cooked
- 1 can (15 oz) chickpeas, drained and rinsed
- 1 cup cherry tomatoes, halved
- 1/2 cucumber, diced
- 1/4 cup red onion, finely chopped
- 1/4 cup Kalamata olives, pitted and sliced
- 2 tablespoons fresh parsley, chopped
- 2 tablespoons feta cheese, crumbled
- 2 tablespoons olive oil
- Juice of 1 lemon
- Salt and pepper to taste

Directions:

1. Preheat the oven to 375°F (190°C).
2. Place bell pepper halves in a baking dish.

3. In a bowl, combine cooked couscous, chickpeas, cherry tomatoes, diced cucumber, red onion, Kalamata olives, fresh parsley, feta cheese, olive oil, lemon juice, salt, and pepper.
4. Stuff each bell pepper half with the couscous mixture.
5. Bake for 20-25 minutes or until peppers are tender.
6. Serve warm.

Nutritional Information:
- Calories: 320 per serving
- Protein: 10g
- Fiber: 8g
- Fat: 12g
- Carbohydrates: 45g

Chickpea and Spinach Coconut Curry

- **Total Time:** 30 minutes
- **Servings:** 4

Ingredients:
- 1 can (15 oz) chickpeas, drained and rinsed
- 2 cups fresh spinach
- 1 onion, chopped
- 2 cloves garlic, minced
- 1 can (14 oz) coconut milk
- 1 tablespoon red curry paste
- 1 teaspoon ground turmeric
- Salt and pepper to taste
- 2 tablespoons olive oil
- Cooked basmati rice for serving

Directions:
1. In a pan, sauté chopped onion and minced garlic in olive oil until softened.
2. Add chickpeas, fresh spinach, coconut milk, red curry paste, ground turmeric, salt, and pepper.
3. Simmer for 15-20 minutes or until spinach is wilted and chickpeas are heated through.
4. Serve over cooked basmati rice.

Nutritional Information:
- Calories: 350 per serving

- Protein: 10g
- Fiber: 8g
- Fat: 20g
- Carbohydrates: 40g

Lemon Herb Roasted Vegetables with Quinoa

- **Total Time:** 45 minutes
- **Servings:** 4

Ingredients:
- 2 cups mixed vegetables (zucchini, bell peppers, cherry tomatoes, etc.)
- 1 cup quinoa, cooked
- 2 tablespoons olive oil
- 2 tablespoons fresh lemon juice
- 1 teaspoon dried thyme
- 1 teaspoon dried rosemary
- Salt and pepper to taste
- Fresh parsley for garnish

Directions:
1. Preheat the oven to 375°F (190°C).
2. In a bowl, toss mixed vegetables with olive oil, fresh lemon juice, dried thyme, dried rosemary, salt, and pepper.
3. Spread the vegetables on a baking sheet in a single layer.
4. Roast in the oven for 30-35 minutes or until vegetables are golden and tender.
5. Serve the roasted vegetables over cooked quinoa.
6. Garnish with fresh parsley.

Nutritional Information:
- Calories: 280 per serving
- Protein: 8g
- Fiber: 8g
- Fat: 10g
- Carbohydrates: 40g

Vegetables

Roasted Brussels Sprouts with Balsamic Glaze

- **Total Time:** 30 minutes
- **Servings:** 4

Ingredients:
- 1 lb Brussels sprouts, trimmed and halved
- 2 tablespoons olive oil
- Salt and pepper to taste
- 2 tablespoons balsamic glaze

Directions:
1. Preheat the oven to 400°F (200°C).
2. Toss Brussels sprouts with olive oil, salt, and pepper.
3. Roast in the oven for 20-25 minutes or until golden and crispy.
4. Drizzle with balsamic glaze before serving.

Nutritional Information:
- Calories: 100 per serving
- Protein: 4g
- Fiber: 5g
- Fat: 7g
- Carbohydrates: 10g

Garlic Lemon Asparagus

- **Total Time:** 15 minutes
- **Servings:** 4

Ingredients:
- 1 lb asparagus, trimmed
- 2 tablespoons olive oil
- 3 cloves garlic, minced
- Zest of 1 lemon
- Salt and pepper to taste

Directions:
1. In a pan, sauté asparagus in olive oil until slightly tender.

2. Add minced garlic and continue to sauté for 2-3 minutes.
3. Sprinkle with lemon zest, salt, and pepper.
4. Serve hot.

Nutritional Information:
- Calories: 60 per serving
- Protein: 3g
- Fiber: 3g
- Fat: 5g
- Carbohydrates: 5g

Turmeric Roasted Cauliflower

- **Total Time:** 25 minutes
- **Servings:** 4

Ingredients:
- 1 head cauliflower, cut into florets
- 2 tablespoons olive oil
- 1 teaspoon turmeric
- 1 teaspoon cumin
- Salt and pepper to taste

Directions:
1. Preheat the oven to 425°F (220°C).
2. Toss cauliflower with olive oil, turmeric, cumin, salt, and pepper.
3. Roast in the oven for 20-25 minutes or until golden brown.

Nutritional Information:
- Calories: 80 per serving
- Protein: 3g
- Fiber: 4g
- Fat: 6g
- Carbohydrates: 7g

Sautéed Kale with Garlic and Lemon

- **Total Time:** 15 minutes
- **Servings:** 4

Ingredients:
- 1 bunch kale, stems removed and leaves chopped
- 2 tablespoons olive oil
- 3 cloves garlic, minced
- Juice of 1 lemon
- Salt and pepper to taste

Directions:
1. In a pan, sauté kale in olive oil until wilted.
2. Add minced garlic and continue to sauté for 2-3 minutes.
3. Drizzle with lemon juice and season with salt and pepper.
4. Serve immediately.

Nutritional Information:
- Calories: 70 per serving
- Protein: 3g
- Fiber: 2g
- Fat: 5g
- Carbohydrates: 8g

Spicy Roasted Broccoli

- **Total Time:** 20 minutes
- **Servings:** 4

Ingredients:
- 1 lb broccoli florets
- 2 tablespoons olive oil
- 1 teaspoon red pepper flakes
- Salt and pepper to taste

Directions:
1. Preheat the oven to 400°F (200°C).
2. Toss broccoli with olive oil, red pepper flakes, salt, and pepper.
3. Roast in the oven for 15-20 minutes or until crispy.

Nutritional Information:
- Calories: 60 per serving
- Protein: 3g
- Fiber: 4g
- Fat: 5g
- Carbohydrates: 8g

Ginger Sesame Stir-Fried Green Beans

- **Total Time:** 15 minutes
- **Servings:** 4

Ingredients:
- 1 lb green beans, trimmed
- 2 tablespoons soy sauce
- 1 tablespoon sesame oil
- 1 tablespoon fresh ginger, minced
- 2 cloves garlic, minced
- 1 tablespoon sesame seeds

Directions:
1. In a wok or pan, stir-fry green beans in sesame oil until slightly tender.
2. Add soy sauce, minced ginger, and minced garlic.
3. Continue to stir-fry for an additional 3-5 minutes.
4. Sprinkle with sesame seeds before serving.

Nutritional Information:
- Calories: 70 per serving
- Protein: 2g
- Fiber: 3g
- Fat: 5g
- Carbohydrates: 7g

Maple Dijon Glazed Carrots

- **Total Time:** 20 minutes
- **Servings:** 4

Ingredients:
- 1 lb carrots, peeled and sliced
- 2 tablespoons maple syrup

- 1 tablespoon Dijon mustard
- 2 tablespoons olive oil
- Salt and pepper to taste
- Fresh parsley for garnish

Directions:
1. Steam or boil carrots until slightly tender.
2. In a bowl, whisk together maple syrup, Dijon mustard, olive oil, salt, and pepper.
3. Toss the cooked carrots in the maple Dijon mixture.
4. Garnish with fresh parsley before serving.

Nutritional Information:
- Calories: 90 per serving
- Protein: 1g
- Fiber: 3g
- Fat: 5g
- Carbohydrates: 12g

Baked Parmesan Zucchini Fries

- **Total Time:** 25 minutes
- **Servings:** 4

Ingredients:
- 2 zucchini, cut into fries
- 1/2 cup grated Parmesan cheese
- 1/2 cup breadcrumbs
- 1 teaspoon garlic powder
- 1 teaspoon dried oregano
- Salt and pepper to taste
- 1 egg, beaten

Directions:
1. Preheat the oven to 425°F (220°C).
2. In a bowl, combine Parmesan cheese, breadcrumbs, garlic powder, dried oregano, salt, and pepper.
3. Dip zucchini fries in beaten egg and then coat them in the Parmesan mixture.
4. Place on a baking sheet and bake for 15-20 minutes or until golden and crispy.

Nutritional Information:
- Calories: 120 per serving

- Protein: 6g
- Fiber: 3g
- Fat: 7g
- Carbohydrates: 10g

Lemon Garlic Roasted Artichokes

- **Total Time:** 40 minutes
- **Servings:** 4

Ingredients:
- 4 artichokes, trimmed and halved
- 2 tablespoons olive oil
- Juice of 2 lemons
- 3 cloves garlic, minced
- Salt and pepper to taste

Directions:
1. Preheat the oven to 375°F (190°C).
2. In a bowl, toss artichoke halves with olive oil, lemon juice, minced garlic, salt, and pepper.
3. Roast in the oven for 30-35 minutes or until tender.

Nutritional Information:
- Calories: 80 per serving
- Protein: 3g
- Fiber: 5g
- Fat: 7g
- Carbohydrates: 10g

Cumin-spiced Roasted Carrots

- **Total Time:** 25 minutes
- **Servings:** 4

Ingredients:
- 1 lb baby carrots
- 2 tablespoons olive oil
- 1 teaspoon ground cumin
- 1 teaspoon smoked paprika
- Salt and pepper to taste
- Fresh cilantro for garnish

Directions:

1. Preheat the oven to 400°F (200°C).
2. Toss baby carrots with olive oil, ground cumin, smoked paprika, salt, and pepper.
3. Roast in the oven for 20-25 minutes or until carrots are caramelized.
4. Garnish with fresh cilantro before serving.

Nutritional Information:

- Calories: 70 per serving
- Protein: 1g
- Fiber: 4g
- Fat: 5g
- Carbohydrates: 8g

Soups and Salads

Tomato Basil Quinoa Soup

- **Total Time:** 40 minutes
- **Servings:** 6

Ingredients:
- 1 cup quinoa, uncooked
- 1 can (28 oz) crushed tomatoes
- 4 cups vegetable broth
- 1 onion, diced
- 3 cloves garlic, minced
- 1 cup fresh basil, chopped
- Salt and pepper to taste

Directions:
1. Rinse quinoa under cold water.
2. In a pot, sauté diced onion and minced garlic until softened.
3. Add crushed tomatoes, vegetable broth, and quinoa. Bring to a simmer.
4. Cook for 20-25 minutes or until quinoa is tender.
5. Stir in chopped basil, salt, and pepper before serving.

Nutritional Information:
- Calories: 220 per serving
- Protein: 8g
- Fiber: 5g
- Fat: 3g
- Carbohydrates: 40g

Avocado and Black Bean Salad

- **Total Time:** 15 minutes
- **Servings:** 4

Ingredients:
- 2 avocados, diced
- 1 can (15 oz) black beans, drained and rinsed
- 1 cup corn kernels, cooked
- 1 cup cherry tomatoes, halved

- 1/4 cup red onion, finely chopped
- 1/4 cup cilantro, chopped
- Juice of 2 limes
- Salt and pepper to taste

Directions:
1. In a bowl, combine diced avocados, black beans, corn, cherry tomatoes, red onion, and cilantro.
2. Drizzle with lime juice and toss gently.
3. Season with salt and pepper before serving.

Nutritional Information:
- Calories: 280 per serving
- Protein: 9g
- Fiber: 12g
- Fat: 14g
- Carbohydrates: 36g

Roasted Red Pepper and Lentil Soup

- **Total Time:** 45 minutes
- **Servings:** 6

Ingredients:
- 1 cup red lentils, rinsed
- 2 red bell peppers, roasted and diced
- 1 onion, chopped
- 3 cloves garlic, minced
- 4 cups vegetable broth
- 1 can (14 oz) diced tomatoes
- 1 teaspoon cumin
- 1 teaspoon smoked paprika
- Salt and pepper to taste

Directions:
1. In a pot, sauté chopped onion and minced garlic until softened.
2. Add red lentils, roasted red peppers, vegetable broth, diced tomatoes, cumin, smoked paprika, salt, and pepper. Bring to a boil.
3. Simmer for 30-35 minutes or until lentils are cooked.
4. Adjust seasoning before serving.

Nutritional Information:
- Calories: 220 per serving
- Protein: 12g
- Fiber: 8g
- Fat: 2g
- Carbohydrates: 40g

Kale and Cranberry Salad with Lemon Vinaigrette

- **Total Time:** 20 minutes
- **Servings:** 4

Ingredients:
- 1 bunch kale, stems removed and leaves chopped
- 1 cup dried cranberries
- 1/2 cup almonds, sliced
- 1/4 cup red onion, thinly sliced
- 1/4 cup feta cheese, crumbled
- Juice of 1 lemon
- 2 tablespoons olive oil
- 1 tablespoon Dijon mustard
- Salt and pepper to taste

Directions:
1. In a bowl, massage kale with lemon juice until slightly wilted.
2. Add dried cranberries, sliced almonds, red onion, and crumbled feta cheese.
3. In a small bowl, whisk together olive oil, Dijon mustard, salt, and pepper.
4. Drizzle the dressing over the salad and toss gently.

Nutritional Information:
- Calories: 250 per serving
- Protein: 6g
- Fiber: 5g
- Fat: 16g
- Carbohydrates: 25g

Butternut Squash and Apple Soup

- **Total Time:** 50 minutes
- **Servings:** 6

Ingredients:

- 1 butternut squash, peeled and diced
- 2 apples, peeled and chopped
- 1 onion, chopped
- 2 cloves garlic, minced
- 4 cups vegetable broth
- 1 teaspoon cinnamon
- 1/2 teaspoon nutmeg
- Salt and pepper to taste
- 1/4 cup coconut milk for garnish

Directions:

1. In a pot, sauté chopped onion and minced garlic until softened.
2. Add diced butternut squash, chopped apples, vegetable broth, cinnamon, nutmeg, salt, and pepper.
3. Bring to a simmer and cook for 30-35 minutes or until squash is tender.
4. Blend the soup until smooth.
5. Serve hot with a swirl of coconut milk.

Nutritional Information:

- Calories: 180 per serving
- Protein: 2g
- Fiber: 5g
- Fat: 1g
- Carbohydrates: 40g

Mediterranean Chickpea Salad

- **Total Time:** 15 minutes
- **Servings:** 4

Ingredients:

- 1 can (15 oz) chickpeas, drained and rinsed
- 1 cucumber, diced
- 1 cup cherry tomatoes, halved
- 1/4 cup red onion, finely chopped

- 1/4 cup Kalamata olives, pitted and sliced
- 1/4 cup feta cheese, crumbled
- 2 tablespoons fresh parsley, chopped
- Juice of 1 lemon
- 2 tablespoons olive oil
- Salt and pepper to taste

Directions:
1. In a bowl, combine chickpeas, diced cucumber, cherry tomatoes, red onion, Kalamata olives, crumbled feta cheese, and chopped fresh parsley.
2. Drizzle with lemon juice and olive oil.
3. Season with salt and pepper before serving.

Nutritional Information:
- Calories: 250 per serving
- Protein: 10g
- Fiber: 8g
- Fat: 10g
- Carbohydrates: 30g

Spinach and Quinoa Salad with Citrus Dressing
- **Total Time:** 20 minutes
- **Servings:** 4

Ingredients:
- 2 cups baby spinach
- 1 cup cooked quinoa
- 1 orange, peeled and segmented
- 1/2 cup pomegranate seeds
- 1/4 cup red onion, thinly sliced
- 1/4 cup almonds, sliced
- Juice of 1 lemon
- 2 tablespoons olive oil
- 1 teaspoon honey
- Salt and pepper to taste

Directions:
1. In a large bowl, combine baby spinach, cooked quinoa, orange segments, pomegranate seeds, sliced red onion, and sliced almonds.
2. In a small bowl, whisk together lemon juice, olive oil, honey, salt, and pepper.
3. Drizzle the dressing over the salad and toss gently.

Nutritional Information:
- Calories: 240 per serving
- Protein: 6g
- Fiber: 6g
- Fat: 10g
- Carbohydrates: 35g

Thai Coconut Curry Pumpkin Soup

- **Total Time:** 40 minutes
- **Servings:** 6

Ingredients:
- 1 can (15 oz) pumpkin puree
- 1 can (14 oz) coconut milk
- 1 onion, chopped
- 2 cloves garlic, minced
- 2 tablespoons red curry paste
- 4 cups vegetable broth
- 1 tablespoon soy sauce
- 1 tablespoon maple syrup
- Salt and pepper to taste
- Fresh cilantro for garnish

Directions:
1. In a pot, sauté chopped onion and minced garlic until softened.
2. Add pumpkin puree, coconut milk, red curry paste, vegetable broth, soy sauce, maple syrup, salt, and pepper.
3. Bring to a simmer and cook for 20-25 minutes.
4. Adjust seasoning and serve hot, garnished with fresh cilantro.

Nutritional Information:
- Calories: 220 per serving
- Protein: 3g
- Fiber: 5g
- Fat: 16g
- Carbohydrates: 20g

Cucumber and Tomato Salad with Herbs

- **Total Time:** 15 minutes
- **Servings:** 4

Ingredients:
- 2 cucumbers, diced
- 2 cups cherry tomatoes, halved
- 1/4 cup red onion, finely chopped
- 1/4 cup fresh mint, chopped
- 1/4 cup fresh parsley, chopped
- Juice of 1 lemon
- 2 tablespoons olive oil
- Salt and pepper to taste

Directions:
1. In a bowl, combine diced cucumbers, cherry tomatoes, chopped red onion, fresh mint, and fresh parsley.
2. Drizzle with lemon juice and olive oil.
3. Season with salt and pepper before serving.

Nutritional Information:
- Calories: 80 per serving
- Protein: 2g
- Fiber: 3g
- Fat: 5g
- Carbohydrates: 10g

Creamy Broccoli and White Bean Soup

- **Total Time:** 30 minutes
- **Servings:** 6

Ingredients:
- 1 lb broccoli, chopped
- 1 can (15 oz) white beans, drained and rinsed
- 1 onion, chopped
- 3 cloves garlic, minced
- 4 cups vegetable broth
- 1 cup unsweetened almond milk
- 2 tablespoons nutritional yeast
- Salt and pepper to taste

Directions:

1. In a pot, sauté chopped onion and minced garlic until softened.
2. Add chopped broccoli, white beans, vegetable broth, almond milk, nutritional yeast, salt, and pepper.
3. Bring to a simmer and cook for 15-20 minutes or until broccoli is tender.
4. Blend the soup until smooth.
5. Adjust seasoning before serving.

Nutritional Information:

- Calories: 180 per serving
- Protein: 8g
- Fiber: 7g
- Fat: 2g
- Carbohydrates: 30g

Snacks

Spicy Roasted Chickpeas

- **Total Time:** 40 minutes
- **Servings:** 4

Ingredients:

- 2 cans (15 oz each) chickpeas, drained and rinsed
- 2 tablespoons olive oil
- 1 teaspoon smoked paprika
- 1/2 teaspoon cayenne pepper
- Salt to taste

Directions:

1. Preheat the oven to 400°F (200°C).
2. Pat chickpeas dry with a paper towel.
3. Toss chickpeas with olive oil, smoked paprika, cayenne pepper, and salt.
4. Roast in the oven for 30-35 minutes or until crispy.

Nutritional Information:

- Calories: 180 per serving
- Protein: 7g
- Fiber: 6g
- Fat: 7g
- Carbohydrates: 25g

Guacamole with Veggie Sticks

- **Total Time:** 15 minutes
- **Servings:** 4

Ingredients:

- 3 avocados, mashed
- 1 tomato, diced
- 1/4 cup red onion, finely chopped
- 1/4 cup cilantro, chopped
- Juice of 1 lime
- Salt and pepper to taste
- Carrot and cucumber sticks for dipping

Directions:
1. In a bowl, combine mashed avocados, diced tomato, chopped red onion, chopped cilantro, lime juice, salt, and pepper.
2. Mix until well combined.
3. Serve with carrot and cucumber sticks.

Nutritional Information:
- Calories: 180 per serving
- Protein: 3g
- Fiber: 9g
- Fat: 15g
- Carbohydrates: 12g

Beet Chips with Yogurt Dip
- **Total Time:** 30 minutes
- **Servings:** 4

Ingredients:
- 2 large beets, thinly sliced
- 2 tablespoons olive oil
- 1/2 teaspoon garlic powder
- 1/2 teaspoon onion powder
- 1/2 teaspoon dried dill
- Salt and pepper to taste
- 1 cup Greek yogurt
- 1 tablespoon honey

Directions:
1. Preheat the oven to 375°F (190°C).
2. Toss beet slices with olive oil, garlic powder, onion powder, dried dill, salt, and pepper.
3. Arrange the slices on a baking sheet and bake for 20-25 minutes or until crispy.
4. In a small bowl, mix Greek yogurt with honey.
5. Serve beet chips with yogurt dip.

Nutritional Information:
- Calories: 120 per serving
- Protein: 6g
- Fiber: 4g
- Fat: 7g
- Carbohydrates: 10g

Edamame and Sea Salt

- **Total Time:** 10 minutes
- **Servings:** 4

Ingredients:

- 2 cups edamame, steamed
- Sea salt to taste

Directions:

1. Steam edamame according to package instructions.
2. Sprinkle it with sea salt and toss to coat.
3. Serve as a simple and nutritious snack.

Nutritional Information:

- Calories: 120 per serving
- Protein: 11g
- Fiber: 8g
- Fat: 5g
- Carbohydrates: 8g

Almond and Coconut Energy Bites

- **Total Time:** 20 minutes
- **Servings:** 12

Ingredients:

- 1 cup almonds, finely chopped
- 1/2 cup shredded coconut
- 1/4 cup almond butter
- 2 tablespoons honey
- 1 teaspoon vanilla extract
- Pinch of salt

Directions:

1. In a bowl, combine chopped almonds, shredded coconut, almond butter, honey, vanilla extract, and a pinch of salt.
2. Mix until the ingredients come together.
3. Roll the mixture into bite-sized balls.
4. Refrigerate for at least 1 hour before serving.

Nutritional Information:
- Calories: 100 per serving
- Protein: 3g
- Fiber: 2g
- Fat: 7g
- Carbohydrates: 8g

Greek Yogurt and Berry Popsicles

- **Total Time:** 4 hours (including freezing time)
- **Servings:** 6

Ingredients:
- 2 cups Greek yogurt
- 1 cup mixed berries (strawberries, blueberries, raspberries)
- 2 tablespoons honey

Directions:
1. In a blender, mix Greek yogurt, mixed berries, and honey until smooth.
2. Pour the mixture into popsicle molds.
3. Insert popsicle sticks and freeze for at least 4 hours.
4. Remove from molds and enjoy.

Nutritional Information:
- Calories: 80 per serving
- Protein: 6g
- Fiber: 1g
- Fat: 2g
- Carbohydrates: 10g

Turmeric Hummus with Whole Grain Crackers

- **Total Time:** 15 minutes
- **Servings:** 6

Ingredients:
- 1 can (15 oz) chickpeas, drained and rinsed
- 2 tablespoons tahini
- 3 tablespoons olive oil
- 1 teaspoon ground turmeric
- 2 cloves garlic, minced

- Juice of 1 lemon
- Salt and pepper to taste
- Whole grain crackers for serving

Directions:

1. In a food processor, blend chickpeas, tahini, olive oil, ground turmeric, minced garlic, lemon juice, salt, and pepper until smooth.
2. Serve with whole grain crackers.

Nutritional Information:

- Calories: 150 per serving
- Protein: 5g
- Fiber: 4g
- Fat: 10g
- Carbohydrates: 12g

Smoked Paprika Roasted Almonds

- **Total Time:** 15 minutes
- **Servings:** 4

Ingredients:

- 2 cups raw almonds
- 1 tablespoon olive oil
- 1 teaspoon smoked paprika
- 1/2 teaspoon cayenne pepper
- Sea salt to taste

Directions:

1. Preheat the oven to 350°F (180°C).
2. Toss raw almonds with olive oil, smoked paprika, cayenne pepper, and sea salt.
3. Spread almonds on a baking sheet and roast for 10-12 minutes or until golden.
4. Let them cool before serving.

Nutritional Information:

- Calories: 200 per serving
- Protein: 7g
- Fiber: 4g
- Fat: 17g
- Carbohydrates: 8g

Sliced Apple with Peanut Butter

- **Total Time:** 5 minutes
- **Servings:** 2

Ingredients:

- 2 apples, sliced
- 4 tablespoons natural peanut butter

Directions:

1. Slice apples into thin wedges.
2. Serve with dollops of natural peanut butter for dipping.

Nutritional Information:

- Calories: 180 per serving
- Protein: 6g
- Fiber: 6g
- Fat: 14g
- Carbohydrates: 15g

Seaweed Snack Rolls

- **Total Time:** 10 minutes
- **Servings:** 4

Ingredients:

- 10 sheets roasted seaweed
- 1 avocado, sliced
- 1 cucumber, julienned
- 1 carrot, julienned
- 1 tablespoon soy sauce
- Sesame seeds for garnish

Directions:

1. Lay out seaweed sheets.
2. Place slices of avocado, julienned cucumber, and julienned carrot along one edge.
3. Roll the seaweed tightly and seal the edge with a little water.
4. Slice into bite-sized rolls and drizzle with soy sauce.
5. Sprinkle with sesame seeds before serving.

Nutritional Information:

- Calories: 80 per serving
- Protein: 2g
- Fiber: 4g
- Fat: 5g
- Carbohydrates: 8g

Desserts

Dark Chocolate Avocado Mousse

- **Total Time:** 15 minutes
- **Servings:** 4

Ingredients:
- 2 ripe avocados
- 1/4 cup cocoa powder
- 1/4 cup maple syrup
- 1 teaspoon vanilla extract
- A pinch of salt
- Dark chocolate shavings for garnish (optional)

Directions:
1. In a blender, combine avocados, cocoa powder, maple syrup, vanilla extract, and a pinch of salt.
2. Blend until smooth and creamy.
3. Spoon the mousse into serving dishes and garnish with dark chocolate shavings if desired.
4. Refrigerate for at least 1 hour before serving.

Nutritional Information:
- Calories: 180 per serving
- Protein: 3g
- Fiber: 7g
- Fat: 14g
- Carbohydrates: 17g

Berry and Coconut Chia Seed Popsicles

- **Total Time:** 4 hours (including freezing time)
- **Servings:** 6

Ingredients:
- 1 cup mixed berries (strawberries, blueberries, raspberries)
- 1 can (14 oz) coconut milk
- 2 tablespoons chia seeds
- 2 tablespoons honey

Directions:

1. In a blender, combine mixed berries, coconut milk, chia seeds, and honey.
2. Blend until well combined.
3. Pour the mixture into popsicle molds.
4. Insert popsicle sticks and freeze for at least 4 hours.
5. Remove from molds and enjoy.

Nutritional Information:

- Calories: 120 per serving
- Protein: 2g
- Fiber: 5g
- Fat: 9g
- Carbohydrates: 10g

Baked Cinnamon Apple Slices

- **Total Time:** 30 minutes
- **Servings:** 4

Ingredients:

- 4 apples, cored and sliced
- 2 tablespoons melted coconut oil
- 1 tablespoon maple syrup
- 1 teaspoon ground cinnamon
- A pinch of nutmeg
- Greek yogurt for serving

Directions:

1. Preheat the oven to 375°F (190°C).
2. In a bowl, toss apple slices with melted coconut oil, maple syrup, ground cinnamon, and nutmeg.
3. Spread the slices on a baking sheet and bake for 20-25 minutes or until tender.
4. Serve with a dollop of Greek yogurt.

Nutritional Information:

- Calories: 150 per serving
- Protein: 1g
- Fiber: 5g
- Fat: 7g
- Carbohydrates: 25g

Vegan Chocolate Chip Cookies

- **Total Time:** 20 minutes
- **Servings:** 12

Ingredients:
- 1 cup almond flour
- 1/4 cup coconut oil, melted
- 1/4 cup maple syrup
- 1 teaspoon vanilla extract
- 1/4 teaspoon baking soda
- A pinch of salt
- 1/2 cup vegan chocolate chips

Directions:
1. Preheat the oven to 350°F (180°C).
2. In a bowl, mix almond flour, melted coconut oil, maple syrup, vanilla extract, baking soda, and a pinch of salt.
3. Fold in vegan chocolate chips.
4. Scoop tablespoon-sized portions onto a baking sheet.
5. Bake for 10-12 minutes or until the edges are golden.
6. Allow to cool before serving.

Nutritional Information:
- Calories: 150 per serving
- Protein: 2g
- Fiber: 2g
- Fat: 12g
- Carbohydrates: 9g

Mango Sorbet with Mint

- **Total Time:** 4 hours (including freezing time)
- **Servings:** 4

Ingredients:
- 2 ripe mangoes, peeled and diced
- 2 tablespoons fresh mint, chopped
- 1/4 cup honey
- Juice of 1 lime

Directions:

1. In a blender, combine diced mangoes, chopped fresh mint, honey, and lime juice.
2. Blend until smooth.
3. Pour the mixture into a shallow dish and freeze for at least 4 hours.
4. Scoop and serve.

Nutritional Information:

- Calories: 120 per serving
- Protein: 1g
- Fiber: 2g
- Fat: 0.5g
- Carbohydrates: 30g

Almond Flour Blueberry Muffins

- **Total Time:** 25 minutes
- **Servings:** 8

Ingredients:

- 2 cups almond flour
- 1/4 cup coconut flour
- 1/4 cup melted coconut oil
- 1/4 cup maple syrup
- 3 eggs
- 1 teaspoon vanilla extract
- 1/2 teaspoon baking soda
- A pinch of salt
- 1 cup fresh blueberries

Directions:

1. Preheat the oven to 350°F (180°C).
2. In a bowl, mix almond flour, coconut flour, melted coconut oil, maple syrup, eggs, vanilla extract, baking soda, and a pinch of salt.
3. Fold in fresh blueberries.
4. Spoon the batter into muffin cups.
5. Bake for 15-18 minutes or until a toothpick comes out clean.

Nutritional Information:

- Calories: 220 per serving
- Protein: 7g
- Fiber: 4g

- Fat: 16g
- Carbohydrates: 15g

Raspberry Coconut Bliss Balls

- **Total Time:** 15 minutes
- **Servings:** 12

Ingredients:
- 1 cup raspberries, fresh or frozen
- 1 cup shredded coconut
- 1/2 cup almond flour
- 2 tablespoons coconut oil, melted
- 2 tablespoons maple syrup
- A pinch of salt

Directions:
1. In a food processor, blend raspberries, shredded coconut, almond flour, melted coconut oil, maple syrup, and a pinch of salt until a dough forms.
2. Roll the mixture into bite-sized balls.
3. Refrigerate for at least 1 hour before serving.

Nutritional Information:
- Calories: 80 per serving
- Protein: 1g
- Fiber: 3g
- Fat: 7g
- Carbohydrates: 6g

Chocolate-Dipped Strawberries

- **Total Time:** 15 minutes
- **Servings:** 4

Ingredients:
- 1 cup strawberries, washed and dried
- 4 oz dark chocolate, melted

Directions:
1. Dip each strawberry into melted dark chocolate, coating them halfway.
2. Place on a parchment-lined tray.
3. Allow the chocolate to set before serving.

Nutritional Information:
- Calories: 80 per serving
- Protein: 1g
- Fiber: 2g
- Fat: 6g
- Carbohydrates: 10g

Lemon Poppy Seed Energy Bites
- **Total Time:** 15 minutes
- **Servings:** 12

Ingredients:
- 1 cup rolled oats
- 1/2 cup almond butter
- 1/4 cup honey
- Zest of 1 lemon
- 1 tablespoon lemon juice
- 1 tablespoon poppy seeds
- A pinch of salt

Directions:
1. In a food processor, blend rolled oats, almond butter, honey, lemon zest, lemon juice, poppy seeds, and a pinch of salt until well combined.
2. Roll the mixture into bite-sized balls.
3. Refrigerate for at least 1 hour before serving.

Nutritional Information:
- Calories: 90 per serving
- Protein: 2g
- Fiber: 2g
- Fat: 5g
- Carbohydrates: 10g

Pumpkin Pie Chia Pudding

- **Total Time:** 4 hours (including chilling time)
- **Servings:** 4

Ingredients:
- 1 cup canned pumpkin puree
- 2 cups almond milk
- 1/4 cup chia seeds
- 2 tablespoons maple syrup
- 1 teaspoon pumpkin pie spice

Directions:
1. In a bowl, whisk together pumpkin puree, almond milk, chia seeds, maple syrup, and pumpkin pie spice.
2. Refrigerate for at least 4 hours or overnight.
3. Stir well before serving.

Nutritional Information:
- Calories: 120 per serving
- Protein: 3g
- Fiber: 8g
- Fat: 5g
- Carbohydrates: 15g

Smoothies

Green Detox Smoothie with Kale and Pineapple

- **Total Time:** 10 minutes
- **Servings:** 2

Ingredients:
- 2 cups kale, stems removed
- 1 cup pineapple chunks
- 1 banana
- 1/2 cucumber, peeled
- 1 tablespoon chia seeds
- 1 cup coconut water
- Ice cubes (optional)

Directions:
1. In a blender, combine kale, pineapple chunks, banana, peeled cucumber, chia seeds, and coconut water.
2. Blend until smooth.
3. Add ice cubes if desired and blend again.
4. Pour into glasses and enjoy!

Nutritional Information:
- Calories: 120 per serving
- Protein: 3g
- Fiber: 8g
- Fat: 2g
- Carbohydrates: 28g

Blueberry Banana Protein Smoothie

- **Total Time:** 5 minutes
- **Servings:** 1

Ingredients:
- 1/2 cup blueberries
- 1 banana
- 1 scoop vanilla protein powder
- 1 tablespoon almond butter

- 1 cup almond milk
- Ice cubes

Directions:
1. In a blender, combine blueberries, banana, vanilla protein powder, almond butter, and almond milk.
2. Blend until smooth.
3. Add ice cubes and blend again.
4. Pour into a glass and enjoy!

Nutritional Information:
- Calories: 300 per serving
- Protein: 20g
- Fiber: 7g
- Fat: 10g
- Carbohydrates: 35g

Tropical Turmeric Smoothie

- **Total Time:** 8 minutes
- **Servings:** 2

Ingredients:
- 1 cup mango chunks
- 1/2 cup pineapple chunks
- 1 banana
- 1 teaspoon turmeric powder
- 1 tablespoon fresh ginger, grated
- 1 cup coconut water
- Ice cubes (optional)

Directions:
1. In a blender, combine mango chunks, pineapple chunks, banana, turmeric powder, grated ginger, and coconut water.
2. Blend until smooth.
3. Add ice cubes if desired and blend again.
4. Pour into glasses and enjoy!

Nutritional Information:
- Calories: 150 per serving
- Protein: 2g

- Fiber: 5g
- Fat: 1g
- Carbohydrates: 38g

Spinach and Berry Smoothie

- **Total Time:** 7 minutes
- **Servings:** 2

Ingredients:
- 2 cups spinach
- 1/2 cup strawberries, hulled
- 1/2 cup blueberries
- 1 banana
- 1 tablespoon flaxseeds
- 1 cup almond milk
- Ice cubes (optional)

Directions:
1. In a blender, combine spinach, strawberries, blueberries, banana, flaxseeds, and almond milk.
2. Blend until smooth.
3. Add ice cubes if desired and blend again.
4. Pour into glasses and enjoy!

Nutritional Information:
- Calories: 120 per serving
- Protein: 3g
- Fiber: 8g
- Fat: 3g
- Carbohydrates: 25g

Mango Ginger Smoothie

- **Total Time:** 6 minutes
- **Servings:** 2

Ingredients:
- 2 cups mango chunks
- 1 tablespoon fresh ginger, grated
- 1/2 cup Greek yogurt

- 1 tablespoon honey
- 1 cup coconut water
- Ice cubes (optional)

Directions:
1. In a blender, combine mango chunks, grated ginger, Greek yogurt, honey, and coconut water.
2. Blend until smooth.
3. Add ice cubes if desired and blend again.
4. Pour into glasses and enjoy!

Nutritional Information:
- Calories: 180 per serving
- Protein: 5g
- Fiber: 3g
- Fat: 1g
- Carbohydrates: 40g

Peach and Almond Milk Smoothie

- **Total Time:** 5 minutes
- **Servings:** 1

Ingredients:
- 1 cup frozen peaches
- 1 banana
- 1/2 cup almond milk
- 1/4 teaspoon almond extract
- 1 tablespoon chia seeds
- Ice cubes

Directions:
1. In a blender, combine frozen peaches, banana, almond milk, almond extract, and chia seeds.
2. Blend until smooth.
3. Add ice cubes and blend again.
4. Pour into a glass and enjoy!

Nutritional Information:
- Calories: 220 per serving
- Protein: 5g

- Fiber: 7g
- Fat: 8g
- Carbohydrates: 35g

Anti-Inflammatory Golden Turmeric Smoothie

- **Total Time:** 8 minutes
- **Servings:** 2

Ingredients:
- 1 cup pineapple chunks
- 1/2 teaspoon ground turmeric
- 1/2 teaspoon ground cinnamon
- 1 banana
- 1 tablespoon chia seeds
- 1 cup coconut water
- Ice cubes (optional)

Directions:
1. In a blender, combine pineapple chunks, ground turmeric, ground cinnamon, banana, chia seeds, and coconut water.
2. Blend until smooth.
3. Add ice cubes if desired and blend again.
4. Pour into glasses and enjoy!

Nutritional Information:
- Calories: 140 per serving
- Protein: 3g
- Fiber: 7g
- Fat: 3g
- Carbohydrates: 30g

Raspberry and Almond Butter Smoothie

- **Total Time:** 7 minutes
- **Servings:** 2

Ingredients:
- 1 cup raspberries
- 1 banana
- 2 tablespoons almond butter

- 1 cup almond milk
- 1 tablespoon honey
- Ice cubes (optional)

Directions:
1. In a blender, combine raspberries, banana, almond butter, almond milk, and honey.
2. Blend until smooth.
3. Add ice cubes if desired and blend again.
4. Pour into glasses and enjoy!

Nutritional Information:
- Calories: 180 per serving
- Protein: 4g
- Fiber: 8g
- Fat: 10g
- Carbohydrates: 24g

Pineapple Mint Cucumber Smoothie

- **Total Time:** 6 minutes
- **Servings:** 2

Ingredients:
- 1 cup pineapple chunks
- 1/2 cucumber, peeled
- 1/4 cup fresh mint leaves
- 1 banana
- 1 tablespoon chia seeds
- 1 cup coconut water
- Ice cubes (optional)

Directions:
1. In a blender, combine pineapple chunks, peeled cucumber, fresh mint leaves, banana, chia seeds, and coconut water.
2. Blend until smooth.
3. Add ice cubes if desired and blend again.
4. Pour into glasses and enjoy!

Nutritional Information:
- Calories: 130 per serving

- Protein: 3g
- Fiber: 7g
- Fat: 2g
- Carbohydrates: 30g

Chocolate Banana Protein Smoothie

- **Total Time:** 5 minutes
- **Servings:** 1

Ingredients:
- 1 banana
- 1 scoop chocolate protein powder
- 1 tablespoon cocoa powder
- 1 tablespoon almond butter
- 1 cup almond milk
- Ice cubes

Directions:
1. In a blender, combine banana, chocolate protein powder, cocoa powder, almond butter, and almond milk.
2. Blend until smooth.
3. Add ice cubes and blend again.
4. Pour into a glass and enjoy!

Nutritional Information:
- Calories: 280 per serving
- Protein: 20g
- Fiber: 7g
- Fat: 11g
- Carbohydrates: 35g

14-Day Meal Plan

Day 1:
- **Breakfast:** Quinoa Breakfast Bowl with Mixed Berries
- **Lunch:** Lentil and Vegetable Stuffed Bell Peppers
- **Dinner:** Eggplant and Spinach Lasagna
- **Snack:** Spicy Roasted Chickpeas
- **Dessert:** Dark Chocolate Avocado Mousse

Day 2:
- **Breakfast:** Vegan Banana Walnut Pancakes
- **Lunch:** Cauliflower and Chickpea Curry
- **Dinner:** Ratatouille with Herbed Quinoa
- **Snack:** Guacamole with Veggie Sticks
- **Dessert:** Berry and Coconut Chia Seed Popsicles

Day 3:
- **Breakfast:** Chia Seed Pudding with Almond Milk and Fresh Fruit
- **Lunch:** Caprese Salad with Balsamic Glaze
- **Dinner:** Stuffed Acorn Squash with Wild Rice
- **Snack:** Beet Chips with Yogurt Dip
- **Dessert:** Baked Cinnamon Apple Slices

Day 4:
- **Breakfast:** Mediterranean Chickpea Scramble
- **Lunch:** Sweet Potato and Quinoa Salad with Lemon Tahini Dressing
- **Dinner:** Vegan Lentil Meatballs with Tomato Sauce
- **Snack:** Edamame and Sea Salt
- **Dessert:** Vegan Chocolate Chip Cookies

Day 5:
- **Breakfast:** Blueberry and Almond Butter Smoothie Bowl
- **Lunch:** Mediterranean Stuffed Eggplant
- **Dinner:** Spicy Thai Basil Eggplant Stir-Fry
- **Snack:** Almond and Coconut Energy Bites
- **Dessert:** Mango Sorbet with Mint

Day 6:
- **Breakfast:** Turmeric Golden Milk Overnight Oats
- **Lunch:** Broccoli and White Bean Soup
- **Dinner:** Butternut Squash and Black Bean Enchiladas
- **Snack:** Greek Yogurt and Berry Popsicles
- **Dessert:** Almond Flour Blueberry Muffins

Day 7:
- **Breakfast:** Spinach and Mushroom Omelette
- **Lunch:** Spinach and Lentil Soup
- **Dinner:** Mediterranean Couscous Stuffed Peppers
- **Snack:** Turmeric Hummus with Whole Grain Crackers
- **Dessert:** Raspberry Coconut Bliss Balls

Day 8:
- **Breakfast:** Mango and Coconut Chia Seed Parfait
- **Lunch:** Vegan Caesar Salad with Crispy Chickpeas
- **Dinner:** Chickpea and Spinach Coconut Curry
- **Snack:** Smoked Paprika Roasted Almonds
- **Dessert:** Chocolate-Dipped Strawberries

Day 9:
- **Breakfast:** Sweet Potato and Black Bean Breakfast Burrito
- **Lunch:** Roasted Vegetable and Quinoa Stuffed Portobello Mushrooms
- **Dinner:** Lemon Herb Roasted Vegetables with Quinoa
- **Snack:** Sliced Apple with Peanut Butter
- **Dessert:** Lemon Poppy Seed Energy Bites

Day 10:
- **Breakfast:** Cinnamon Raisin Quinoa Porridge
- **Lunch:** Pesto Zucchini Noodles with Cherry Tomatoes
- **Dinner:** Chickpea and Avocado Salad
- **Snack:** Seaweed Snack Rolls
- **Dessert:** Pumpkin Pie Chia Pudding

Day 11:
- **Breakfast:** Green Pea and Mint Frittata
- **Lunch:** Cauliflower and Chickpea Tacos
- **Dinner:** Vegan Lentil Meatballs with Tomato Sauce
- **Snack:** Spicy Roasted Chickpeas
- **Dessert:** Dark Chocolate Avocado Mousse

Day 12:
- **Breakfast:** Vegan Banana Walnut Pancakes
- **Lunch:** Greek Salad with Chickpea Patties
- **Dinner:** Eggplant and Spinach Lasagna
- **Snack:** Guacamole with Veggie Sticks
- **Dessert:** Berry and Coconut Chia Seed Popsicles

Day 13:
- **Breakfast:** Chia Seed Pudding with Almond Milk and Fresh Fruit
- **Lunch:** Sweet Potato and Quinoa Salad with Lemon Tahini Dressing
- **Dinner:** Vegan Lentil Meatballs with Tomato Sauce
- **Snack:** Edamame and Sea Salt
- **Dessert:** Baked Cinnamon Apple Slices

Day 14:
- **Breakfast:** Blueberry and Almond Butter Smoothie Bowl
- **Lunch:** Spinach and Feta Stuffed Mushrooms
- **Dinner:** Butternut Squash and Black Bean Enchiladas
- **Snack:** Almond and Coconut Energy Bites
- **Dessert:** Mango Sorbet with Mint

Conclusion

As you reach the conclusion of this journey towards a Vegetarian Anti-Inflammatory Lifestyle, take a moment to reflect on the transformative experiences you've encountered throughout this exploration of flavors, nutrients, and wellness. The culmination of these recipes, carefully crafted to nourish your body and soothe inflammation, marks not just the end of a guide but the beginning of a sustained commitment to your well-being.

Your culinary adventure has not merely been a sequence of recipes but a transformative experience. You've delved into the world of plant-based, anti-inflammatory nutrition, unlocking the potential of vegetables, fruits, grains, and legumes to heal and nourish. By embracing this lifestyle, you've harnessed the power of food as medicine, understanding how each ingredient contributes to your overall health.

Consider the changes you've witnessed, not only in your physical health but in your energy levels, mood, and overall vitality. Perhaps you've noticed a reduction in inflammation, improved digestion, or a newfound sense of balance. These changes are not just a testament to the effectiveness of a vegetarian, anti-inflammatory diet but also to your commitment to embracing a holistic approach to health.

Take note of the flavors that have become your allies in this journey. The vibrant, nutrient-packed meals you've indulged in are not just sustenance; they are a celebration of the diverse and delicious offerings nature provides. From the earthy richness of lentils to the sweet freshness of berries, each ingredient has played a role in enhancing your well-being.

Remember, this isn't the end; it's a continuation of the positive changes you've initiated. The Vegetarian Anti-Inflammatory Lifestyle is not a temporary fix but a profound shift towards a healthier, more balanced life. With each mindful meal, you are nurturing not just your body but also the roots of a lasting well-being that will flourish in the seasons to come. Your journey towards wellness is a lifelong adventure, and as you step into the future, let the lessons learned and the flavors experienced guide you towards a sustained and vibrant well-being.

Made in the USA
Monee, IL
04 January 2025

76009514R10050